Oh My Darling, ♫ Porcupine ♪

And Other Silly Sing-Along Songs

Created by
Bruce Lansky

Illustrated by
Stephen Carpenter

Meadowbrook Press
Distributed by Simon & Schuster
New York

Library of Congress Cataloging-in-Publication Data

Oh my darling, porcupine : and other silly sing-along songs/ created by Bruce Lansky ; illustrations and cover art, Stephen Carpenter.
       p. cm.
   Summary:"A collection of silly new lyrics to kids' favorite sing-along songs"—Provided by publisher.
   ISBN 0-88166-496-0
   1. Children's songs—Texts. I. Lansky, Bruce. II. Carpenter, Stephen, ill.
   ML54.6.O36 2006
   782.42164'0268—dc22

2005020709

Editorial Director: Christine Zuchora-Walske
Coordinating Editor and Copyeditor: Angela Wiechmann
Production Manager: Paul Woods
Graphic Design Manager: Tamara Peterson
Illustrations and Cover Art: Stephen and Tad Carpenter

Published by Meadowbrook Press, 5451 Smetana Drive, Minnetonka, Minnesota 55343

www.meadowbrookpress.com

BOOK TRADE DISTRIBUTION by Simon and Schuster, a division of Simon and Schuster, Inc.,
1230 Avenue of the Americas, New York, New York 10020

12 11 10 09 08 07 06   10 9 8 7 6 5 4 3 2 1

Printed in China

Credits

"Oh My Darling, Porcupine" copyright © 2006 by Steve Charney;"Row, Row, Row Your Boat" (third stanza) copyright © 1994 by Bill Dodds, previously published in *A Bad Case of the Giggles*;"Tinkle, Tinkle, Little Cat" copyright © 2006 by Kathy Kenney-Marshall;"Bring Back My Sister to Me," "Cattle in Kitchens," "Clean Your Bedroom," "I Like to Wear My T-shirt," and "This Hand Is My Hand" copyright © 2006 by Bruce Lansky;"Yankee Doodle" copyright © 2006 by Bruce Lansky, based on poems previously published in *Mary Had a Little Jam*;"I Wonder Why…" copyright © 2006 by Bruce Lansky, based on poems previously published in *Funny Little Poems for Funny Little People*;"Row, Row, Row Your Boat" (first and second stanzas) copyright © 2006 by Bruce Lansky, based on a poem previously published in *Peter, Peter, Pizza-Eater*;"Take Me Out of the Ballgame" copyright © 2006 by Jeff Nathan;"Polly Ann from Tallahassee" and "Grover Can Whimper" copyright © 2006 by Eric Ode;"Give Me Lots and Lots of Candy" and "Take Me Out to the Mall, Mom" copyright © 2006 by A. Maria Plover;"The Top of My Hot Dog" copyright © 2006 by Robert Pottle;"Tinkle, Tinkle, Little Bat" copyright © 2004 by Dianne Rowley, previously published in *Rolling in the Aisles*;"My Older Brother Bob" copyright © 2006 by Robert Scotellaro; and "Santa Claus Is Hungry Tonight" copyright © 2006 by Timothy Tocher. All songs used with permission of the authors.

Acknowledgments

Many thanks to the following teachers and their students who tested songs for this anthology: Mark Benthall, Lakeway Elementary, Austin, TX; Hillary Coombes, Deer Creek Elementary, Crowley, TX; Sandra Kane, Lincoln Elementary, Fairbault, MN; Kathy Kenney-Marshall, McCarthy Elementary, Framingham, MA; Carol Larson, Rum River Elementary, Andover, MN; Teri Lifer, Butler Elementary, Butler, OH; Jenny Myer, East Elementary, New Richmond, WI; Susie Olsen, Lincoln Elementary, Fairbault, MN; James Parr, McCarthy Elementary, Framingham, MA; John Pundsack, East Elementary, New Richmond, WI; Ruth Refsnider, East Elementary, New Richmond, WI; Cathy Rodrigue, Deer Creek Elementary, Crowley, TX; Connie Roetzer, East Elementary, New Richmond, WI; Beverly Semanko, Rum River Elementary, Andover, MN; Suzanne Storbeck, Holy Name School, Wayzata, MN; Carleen Tjader, East Elementary, New Richmond, WI; and Julie White, East Elementary, New Richmond, WI.

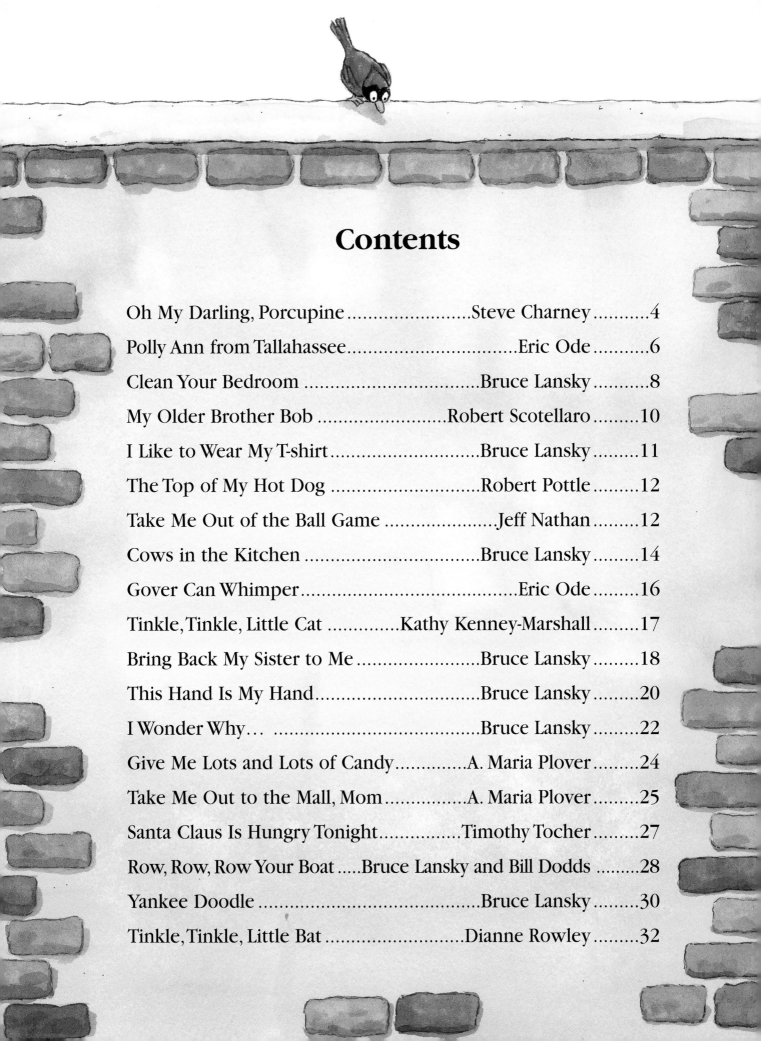

Contents

Oh My Darling, Porcupine

(sing to the tune of "Clementine")

I was standing in a forest
underneath a tree of pine.
There I spied my future bride, and
how I wished that she were mine.

Oh my darling, oh my darling, oh my darling, porcupine.
You are lost and gone forever. Dreadful sorry, porcupine.

And my darling, she was snarling—
should have seen that as a sign.
To impress her and caress her
was a big mistake of mine.

Oh my darling, oh my darling, oh my darling, porcupine.
You are lost and gone lost forever. Dreadful sorry, porcupine.

I was standing in a forest
underneath a tree of pine.
Now I'm sobbing, my hand's throbbing.
Anyone got iodine?

Oh my darling, oh my darling, oh my darling, porcupine.
You are lost and gone forever, but at least your quills are mine.

Steve Charney

4

Polly Ann from Tallahassee

(sing to the tune of "Did You Ever See a Lassie")

Polly Ann from Tallahassee
was sassy and brassy.
Polly thought she was so classy
with bows on her hat.
A bird saw that bonnet
and dove down upon it.
So unlucky for that lassie,
her hat is now flat.

Polly rode upon a turkey
to see Albuquerque.
Polly thought it would be quirky
to work at the zoo.
Her hat and its ribbons
were stolen by gibbons,
so she ran from Albuquerque
to Park Avenue.

Polly sailed to Tijuana
upon a piranha.
Polly found an old iguana
asleep on her head.
It snored very sweetly
and fit so completely,
Polly traded in her hat
for that reptile instead.

Eric Ode

6

Clean Your Bedroom

(sing to the tune of "Alouette")

"Clean your bedroom."
Mom says, "Clean your bedroom."
"Clean your bedroom."
She says it every day.

"Pick your clothes up off the floor.
Make your bed, then shut the door."
"Make your bed." (*Make your bed*.)
"Clean your room." (*Clean your room*.)
Ohhhhhhh!

8

"Wash the dishes."
Mom says, "Wash the dishes."
"Wash the dishes."
She says it every day.

"Wash the dishes—dry them, too.
Stack them up, then you'll be through."
"Wash them up." (*Wash them up*.)
"Dry them up." (*Dry them up*.)
Ohhhhhhh!

"Do your homework."
Dad says, "Do your homework."
"Do your homework."
He says it every day.

"Do your homework, then have fun.
No TV until you're done."
"No TV." (*No TV*.)
"Till you're done." (*Till you're done*.)
Ohhhhhhh!

Bruce Lansky

9

My Older Brother Bob

(sing to the tune of "Ta-Ra-Ra Boom-De-Ay"
or "The Farmer in the Dell")

My older brother Bob
is an enormous slob.
He leaves his underwear
all scattered here and there.

You really could fill up
a giant garbage truck
with all the food he drops
and spills and drips and plops.

His socks stink up his room.
They'd cause a skunk to swoon.
He leaves them in a mound—
the flies all buzz around.

I wish he would consent
to live inside a tent.
It wouldn't be that hard.
We'd keep it in the yard.

Ta-ra-ra boom-de-ay,
that day will come, I pray.
But till my brother's gone,
I'll keep my gas mask on!

Robert Scotellaro

I Like to Wear a T-Shirt

(sing to the tune of "Pink Pajamas")

I like to wear a T-shirt when I'm walking down the street.
I wear a belt on my blue jeans to keep me looking neat.
But when my clothes are in the wash, and nothing's left to wear,
I wrap a towel around my waist so neighbors will not stare.
Glory, glory hallelujah! My clothes are dirty, what's it to ya?
When my clothes are in the wash and nothing's left to wear,
I wrap a towel around my waist so neighbors will not stare.

Bruce Lansky

The Top of My Hot Dog

(sing to the tune of "On Top of Old Smoky")

The top of my hot dog
is no longer bare.
It now has a topping
I didn't want there.

I ordered my hot dog.
I ordered it plain,
without any toppings.
I ordered in vain.

Well, I started eating,
then looked in the air.
A seagull few toward me
and gave me a scare.

I covered my hot dog
a second too late.
What fell from that seagull's
too gross to relate.

The top of my hot dog
is no longer bare.
It now has a topping
a seagull put there.

Robert Pottle

Take Me Out of the Ball Game

(sing to the tune of "Take Me Out to the Ball Game")

Take me out of the ball game.
Take me off of the mound.
Get me out quickly—oh, please don't wait.
I throw hard, but I can't reach home plate.
I just walked another four runs in.
If we don't win, I'm to blame.
And it's one, two, three strikes, I'm out
when I play this game.

Take me out of the ball game.
Take me out right away.
Why did you put me at second base?
Every hit makes me cover my face.
I just broke the record for errors.
If we don't win, I'm to blame.
And it's one, two, three strikes, I'm out
when I play this game.

Take me out of the ball game.
Take me out of right field.
Put someone in who won't trip and fall—
anyone who can catch a fly ball.
Now I just missed my fourteenth grounder.
If we don't win, I'm to blame.
And it's one, two, three strikes, I'm out
when I play this game.

Take me out of the ball game.
It's my turn up at bat.
I swing and miss, but it's no surprise.
I'm too frightened to open my eyes.
And I heard strike three whizzing past me.
If we don't win, I'm to blame.
For it's one, two, three strikes, I'm out
when I play this game.

Jeff Nathan

Cows in the Kitchen

(sing to the tune of "Oh, Susanna")

I was on a ranch in Texas,
and I got a big surprise.
There were no cows in the kitchen,
but they sure made lots of pies.

Down in Texas
I got a big surprise.
There were no cows in the kitchen,
but they sure made lots of pies.

And the raisins in the garden
were not fit for me to eat.
They did not fall from a grapevine;
they were just a rabbit's treat.

Lots of raisins,
but none were fit to eat.
They did not fall from a grapevine;
they were just a rabbit's treat.

When I looked out of the window
there was not much I could see.
Too much whitewash on the window.
Had the birds all aimed at me?

Through the window
there wasn't much to see.
Too much whitewash on the window.
Had the birds all aimed at me?

Bruce Lansky

Grover Can Whimper

(sing to the tune of "Over the River and through the Wood")

Grover can whimper and lick your face.
He'll stretch, and he'll fetch your shoe.
He knows how to stay, to sit, and to lay,
and to howl and growl on cue.

Grover can nuzzle and pant and bay.
He sniffs, and he digs a hole.
He sheds and heels and gulps his meals
and drinks from the toilet bowl.

Grover can piddle. He yips and fights.
He bites at the postman's legs.
He nips at the gnats and chases the cats.
He pants and barks and begs.

Grover rolls over to scratch a flea.
I guarantee it's true.
To get your kicks, come see the tricks
my brother has learned to do.

Eric Ode

Tinkle, Tinkle, Little Cat

(sing to the tune of "Twinkle, Twinkle, Little Star")

Tinkle, tinkle, little cat.
Why'd you mess the floor like that?
Mom just used her brand-new mop.
Kitty cat, you'd better stop.
What goes on inside your head?
Use your litter box instead!

Naughty, naughty, little cat.
Why'd you scratch the couch like that?
Then you scratched up Dad's new chair.
Our clean laundry's everywhere.
Even though I love you most,
next time use your scratching post.

Sprinkle, sprinkle, rug shampoo.
What's a kid like me to do?
When you make a mess like that,
you are such a naughty cat.
Mom says if you mess once more,
kitty cat goes out the door!

Kathy Kenney-Marshall

Bring Back My Sister to Me

(sing to the tune of "My Bonnie")

My sister woke up in the morning.
She had to go potty real bad.
My father had just left the seat up.
She fell in the toilet, how sad.

Bring back, bring back,
please bring back my sister to me, to me.
Bring back, bring back,
please bring back my sister to me.

My brother went into the bathroom.
He carried his new fishing pole.
He cast his line into the toilet.
A fish pulled him into the bowl.

Bring back, bring back,
please bring back my brother to me, to me.
Bring back, bring back,
please bring back my brother to me.

The toilet just never stops running.
The toilet tank float caused a leak.
My dad slipped while fixing the floater.
Poor Daddy is now up the creek!

Bring back, bring back,
please bring back my daddy to me, to me.
Bring back, bring back,
please bring back my daddy to me.

Mom noticed the john overflowing.
She grabbed an old plunger and ran.
The plunger broke while she was plunging.
That's how she wound up in the can.

Bring back, bring back,
please bring back my mommy to me, to me.
Bring back, bring back,
please bring back my mommy to me.

Last seen on the seat of the toilet,
our kitty was chasing a mouse.
Our cat lost her balance and fell in.
Her "MEOW!" could be heard through the house.

Bring back, bring back,
please bring back our kitty to me, to me.
Bring back, bring back,
please bring back our kitty to me.

My dog took a drink from the toilet.
He stood with his paws on the ground.
He leaned over into the toilet.
He fell in and just about drowned.

Bring back, bring back,
please bring back my doggy to me, to me.
Bring back, bring back,
please bring back my doggy to me.

Bruce Lansky

This Hand Is My Hand
(sing to the tune of "This Land Is My Land")

This hand is my hand.
It isn't your hand.
The thought of your touch
is what I can't stand.
And being near you
is not what I planned.
This hand was made for me, not you.

This hair is my hair.
It isn't your hair.
My hair is one thing
that I will not share.
So if you touch it
my friends will all stare.
This hair was made for me, not you.

These cheeks are my cheeks.
They are not your cheeks.
So please don't kiss them,
because your breath reeks.
I'd rather be kissed
by twenty math geeks.
These cheeks were made for me, not you.

These lips are my lips.
They are not your lips.
I'll never kiss you,
because your nose drips.
If you get near me
I'll do ten backflips.
These lips were made for me, not you.

Bruce Lansky

I Wonder Why...

(sing to the tune of "My Bonnie")

Boys
I wonder why girls were invented.
They spend so much time on their hair.
If they were as bald as my grandpa,
the mirror would give them a scare.

Girls
I wonder why boys were invented.
They're dirty and messy and rude.
They never wash up before dinner
and burp after eating their food.

Bruce Lansky

Give Me Lots and Lots of Candy

(sing to the tune of "I'm a Yankee Doodle Dandy")

Give me lots and lots of candy
when I'm at the grocery store.
Miles of aisles filled with lollipops,
jawbreakers, fruit chews galore.
I'll stuff my cart with peanut clusters,
pile gumballs to the sky.

At the checkout I'll grab roll-ups.
They're two for a dollar.
Candy is what I love to buy!

Give me lots and lots of candy.
That is what I love to eat.
For breakfast, bowls of crunchy chocolate bars—
chewy and gooey and sweet.
A lunch time pizza would be tasty
made with fudge and gummi fish.

And for dinner, I'll take seconds
if the beans are jelly.
Candy's my very favorite dish!

A. Maria Plover

Take Me Out to the Mall, Mom
(sing to the tune of "Take Me Out to the Ball Game")

Take me out to the mall, Mom.
Take me out to the mall.
Buy me some flip-flops, a purse, and tees.
Can I get my ears pierced—oh, Mom, please?
When it's time to eat, there's the food court.
We'll buy CDs on the way.
We can shop, shop, shop till we drop
at the mall today!

Take me out to the mall, Mom.
Take me out to the mall.
I need nail polish, lip-gloss, hair gel.
If I can't get my ears pierced, oh well!
Look at these cool jeans—aren't they awesome?
I need a new pair or two.
Love to shop, shop, shop till we drop
at the mall with you!

A. Maria Plover

Santa Claus Is Hungry Tonight

(sing to the tune of "Santa Claus Is Coming to Town")

Oh, you better get up
and make something quick.
It wouldn't be smart
to starve old Saint Nick.
Santa Claus is hungry tonight.

Your mom saved him some ice cream
and a slice of pumpkin pie.
Too bad you finished both of them
while he was flying 'cross the sky.

Oh, you needed a snack
and didn't think twice.
You ate Santa's treats,
so now pay the price.
Santa Claus is hungry tonight.

He knows you are not sleeping.
Your snoring is so fake.
You'd better get yourself downstairs
and bake the man a cake.

Oh, you better get up
and make something quick.
It wouldn't be smart
to starve old Saint Nick.
Santa Claus is hungry tonight.

Timothy Tocher

Row, Row, Row Your Boat
(sing to the tune of "Row, Row, Row Your Boat")

Row, row, row your boat,
gently down the creek.
You might get your bottom wet
if you spring a leak.

Row, row, row your boat,
gently 'round the lake.
Don't stand up and rock the boat.
That's a big mistake.

Row, row, row your boat,
gently down the stream,
until you hit the waterfall—
then you'll start to scream. *Aaaiiieee!*

Bruce Lansky and Bill Dodds

Yankee Doodle

(sing to the tune of "Yankee Doodle")

Yankee Doodle went to town
riding on a chicken.
He went into a restaurant
and came out finger lickin'.

Chorus
Yankee Doodle couldn't ride
to town upon his pony.
The pony had a tummy ache
from too much bad baloney.

Yankee Doodle went to town
riding on a rooster.
His saddle wasn't high enough.
He had to get a booster.

Chorus

Yankee Doodle went to town
riding on a monkey.
He had to take a shower quick
because he smelled so funky.

Chorus

Yankee's mother went to town
riding on a gator.
She didn't feed the gator so
the hungry gator ate 'er.

Chorus

Bruce Lansky

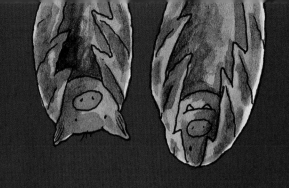

Tinkle, Tinkle, Little Bat
(sing to the tune of "Twinkle, Twinkle, Little Star")

Tinkle, tinkle, little bat.
Wonder where the potty's at?

Straight ahead or to the right?
Caves are very dark at night.

Little bat, why do you frown?
Did you tinkle upside down?

Dianne Rowley